THE IMPOSSIBLE TAKES A LITTLE LONGER

A history of Israel in Political Cartoons
from the Yom Kippur War through
the Lebanon Campaign

by

Noah Bee

Text by
Yehuda Lev

BLOCH PUBLISHING COMPANY ● NEW YORK

International Standard Book No. 0-8197-0491-1
Library of Congress Catalogue No. 83-71041
Copyright © Noah M. Bee
Printed in the United States of America

To Carmi, Harriet, Sharon and David
who make life meaningful

Acknowledgements

I would like to take this opportunity to thank all those who helped me make this volume come to fruition. Foremost is the editor-in-chief of the Jewish Telegraphic Agency,* Murray Zuckoff with whom I discuss the subject of the next cartoon almost every week. His clear thinking contributes to the quality and orderly sequence of events and enable me to foresee what might happen two weeks later when the cartoon appears in the press. It is not an easy problem in view of the fast moving world events. My gratitude also goes to my friend Yehuda Lev who undertook to write the chronological text of the last nine years and the captions for each cartoon. This was done in spite of the divergence of our political views. Thanks to Ron Solomon for his help. I would like to mention my good friend Ernest Barbarash who gave me my first cartoon break after arriving in the U.S.A. And last, but not least, bouquets to my wife Marian, who prepared my manuscripts, was my judge and stood by me all the way.

*Some of the cartoons appeared in other publications, among them Israel Today.

FOREWORD

In the foreword to my book "In Spite of Everything," published in 1973, I wrote that "The events of the past 25 years in the State of Israel have been filled with progress, dynamism and guts." No one could foresee that the following October the course of history would take a different turn.

The Yom Kippur War of 1973 opened a Pandora's Box of perils, generated by the new petro-powers of the Middle East. Their shadows continue to hang over the west and things are more ominous because of the political union of these petty tyrannies with the states of the Soviet bloc. They now form a Communist-Third World majority that dominates international organizations. In their vocabularies Israel, once the David of the Middle East conflict, has become its Goliath, the "lackey of American imperialism and colonialism."

The journey to Jerusalem of Egyptian president Anwar Sadat broke the unanimity of this anti-Israel cabal of totalitarian states. Sadat was the sole Arab leader to have the courage to attempt to find a peaceful rather than a military solution to the Arab-Israel conflict. As of this writing, with Sadat murdered, the Sinai back in Egyptian hands, the Palestine problem as far as ever from a solution and deep rifts among the Arab nations being exploited to the utmost by the Soviet Union, no one can foretell whether or not Sadat's mission will result in a stable and permanent peace between Israel and Egypt.

Whatever the eventual outcome there is no doubt but that Sadat's initiative and all of the negotiations that have so far followed from it, are the most important developments to have affected Israel in the years since the Yom Kippur War.

Throughout the Camp David meetings I remained skeptical about Sadat's sincerity, conditioned as I was by decades of anti-Israel policy and propaganda by successive Egyptian rulers. But Sadat's record, to the moment that he died in a hail of bullets fired by Moslem fundamentalist fanatics, was that of a man of peace, once he determined that peace was necessary for Egypt's economic and social progress. In taking this stand, in contrast to the policies of the other Arab states, Sadat accomplished two principal objectives; the return of the Sinai to Egyptian control and the persuasion of American political and military leaders that Egypt must become the cornerstone of a strong American military posture for the Middle East. The consequences of this latter development are not yet evident to us but what is clear is that Israel's influence in the formation of American Middle East policy has decreased while that of the Saudis and Egyptians has increased.

Ever since the Vietnam War thinking in the Pentagon has taken a radical change in that reliance on conventional forces took a back seat in favor of a nuclear deterrent. It was obvious that sooner or later this trend would echo in the Middle East. In this process, Israel, a military land power lost its glamor as a strategic ally. Besides, Sadat gave the U.S. an alternative by making Egypt available to American strategic interests. Now with Sadat gone and the Sinai returned to Egypt, the question is: "what comes next?" And now a new element has been brought into the picture—the Saudi Arabians.

The Saudis, a royal family and its many courtiers, who have the luck to sit on a treasure in oil unsurpassed anywhere, have become the golden calf of the western world. Through their OPEC cartel they carry great weight in the name of Allah and petro-dollars. These are the same Saudis who declare a Jihad (holy war) against Israel, who support every radical Arab cause and especially the PLO with their dollars, and who are labeled "moderates" by the west. They are doing everything they can to bring Egypt back into the Arab fold and to destroy the peace with Israel.

In his most recent book "Why We Were in Vietnam," Norman Podhoretz points to the moral failure exhibited by the United States in its relations with the South Vietnamese when it abandoned them to their conquerors. What will happen, when push comes to shove, if the United States is called upon to make similar decisions regarding its obligations to Israel? When the Reagan Administration came to power it planned to create an anti-Soviet bloc in the Middle East consisting of Egypt, Saudi Arabia, Sudan, Jordan and Israel. But the plan never got off the ground because the Saudis regard Israel, not the Soviet Union, as their principal enemy.

The question "What happens next?" was answered on June 6th when Israeli soldiers moved into southern Lebanon, across a border which, through the years, had been the site of numerous terrorist attacks on Israeli towns and settlements in northern Galilee. In spite of a brilliant military campaign which saw its forces move to the suburbs of Beirut, Israel paid a heavy price both in casualties and in her political relations with other countries. American pressure on Israel not to enter Beirut itself enabled the PLO terrorists in the city to recover from their defeats and find refuge among the civilian population.

Only after tremendous pressure from Israeli air raids, the PLO forces agreed to leave the city and were scattered to different Arab countries. A short while after the newly elected president of Lebanon, Bashir Gemayel, a Maronite Christian, was assassinated by Moslems. What followed was a massacre in two Palestinian camps in Beirut conducted by the Falangists, who wanted to avenge the killing of their leader. Because Israel had assumed responsibility for the civilian population in the city, world media accused Israel for the responsibility of the massacre. This campaign assumed ugly proportions and every hater of the Jewish state from the extreme left to the right had a heavy heyday. Under great pressure from Israeli public opinion the government set up a commission of inquiry.

"Operation Peace for Galilee" whether it caught the American government by surprise or not, resulted in a tremendous rise of U.S. prestige in the area and gave the Soviets a bloody nose. Riding on the tide of this popularity, President Reagan came out with his own plan for a Middle East peace. In retrospect, it can be stated that Israel showed the world that sometimes it is

9

necessary to use military force to deal with the scourge of terrorism. The strong reaction on the part of the western world to the events was envy and embarrassment that little Israel had the guts to do it. It reminds one of the comment the former British Prime Minister Harold MacMillian made when asked about Britain's future, who said, "The future I hope for Britain is more like that of Israel. In June, 1967, while the world debated, Israel's three millions imposed their will on their enemies. They did it with what any great people need—resolution, courage, determination and pride. These are the things that count in men and in nations."

By the close of the year Israel and Lebanon were engaged in hard bargaining with the United States taking the role of mediator. Egypt sits on the sidelines, hardening its attitude toward Israel in order to curry favor with the Saudis. The Americans are leaning on Israel to grant more concessions and Israel is hardpressed to resist all of this pressure.

If there is to be peace, the "moderate" Arab states will have to get it into their craniums that as long as they persist in the idea of a military solution "some time in the future", peace in that part of the world will remain just a dream.

What can we expect to be the subject of a third volume in this series, published perhaps in another half dozen years? We cannot, of course, be certain, but looking in a Middle East crystal ball, cracked perhaps by the heat of anger and the winds of invective, we can foresee a very rough time ahead for Israel. Her borders have shrunk and she is more and more subject to the pressures that could bring about another explosion.

For 2,000 years the Jewish people lived at the mercy or on the tolerance of others. Ever since May 14, 1948, they have been the masters of their own destiny, in their own land. Whatever happens in the future will depend very much on the wisdom, patience and guts of those who guide that destiny.

It was David Ben Gurion who said that "It is not important what others say about us. What is important is what we shall do."

—Noah Bee

From
the Yom Kippur War
through the
Lebanon Campaign

1973

In Israel it was called "The Earthquake" and never was a name more aptly chosen for a military assault. The unexpected fury of the Egyptian-Syrian Yom Kippur war against Israel and the widespread destruction that it caused, shook the nation to its very foundations. By the evening of Yom Kippur, a day that had begun with the customary peaceful call to prayer and penitence, the people of Israel were girding for the defense of their land.

In Jewish communities everywhere and especially in those of the free world, emergency measures were taken to provide Israel with the support she would require to survive. Thousands of young men and women filled the aircraft bound for Tel Aviv, volunteering to replace workers now at the front. Tens of millions of dollars were contributed to bolster Israel's economy, political leaders were lobbied on Israel's behalf and the general community was kept informed about Israel's position on the issues of the Middle East.

The combat ended with Israel victorious on the battlefield but in serious trouble both internally and externally. In Jerusalem questions were raised about how it had been possible for Egypt and Syria to have mounted a surprise attack, and investigations were promised. Internationally the Arabs were able to wield the oil weapon with such effectiveness that with the exception of the United States virtually every one of Israel's traditional friends either broke off diplomatic relations or held off from offering assistance.

At year's end, Israelis prepared to go to the polls in a national election even as they mourned the death of the founder of their country, David Ben Gurion. The shooting had ended and the negotiations with the Syrians and Egyptians were about to begin. The aftershocks continued but the earthquake was now history.

October 7, 1973
As Israel prayed, Yom Kippur 5933, her
enemies moved to the attack, striking with
devastating surprise. Suddenly the nation
was engulfed in a two front war.

The Jews of the world rallied to Israel's defense with financial, political, and physical support.

October 12, 1973

For the first several days it appeared that the Arabs might attain their objectives. But the Israel Defense Forces mobilized, counter-attacked, and carried the war into Egypt and Syria.

October 19, 1973

SITTING "PRETTY"

SPIRIT OF MUNICH

NATO ALLIES

'73 Bee

October 26, 1973

The Arab use of oil, withdrawing it from nations which sided with Israel or which preferred to remain neutral, proved effective. Even America's NATO allies joined in blockading Israel, fearing the loss of their energy sources.

—WILL HE MAKE IT BACK?

MASSIVE SOVIET HELP

THIRD WORLD

SOME NATO ALLIES

UNITED NATIONS

SUEZ

SADAT

YOM KIPPUR WAR

'73 Bee

Both the Americans and the Soviets intervened to save the trapped Arab armies. Support was particularly strong for Anwar Sadat's government.

November 2, 1973

November 9, 1973

Even while the guns were still firing, questions were asked in Israel about the misconceptions about Arab strength which the Israeli government and the military both held before the Yom Kippur War.

THE CHEERING SECTION

KEEP IT UP, FAISAL!

ARAB OIL.

November 16, 1973

It soon became obvious that the big winner in the oil struggle was the Soviet Union which had plenty of oil of its own and which encouraged the Arabs in their blockade of the west.

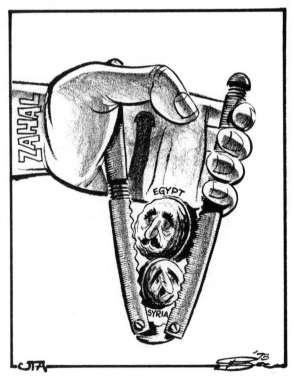

ZAHAL

EGYPT

SYRIA

Israel's advances towards Cairo and Damascus in the closing days of the fighting demonstrated the superiority of its military strength.

November 23, 1973

November 30, 1973

The death of Israel's first Prime Minister,
David Ben Gurion, recalled for Israelis
earlier times of trial from which the nation
had emerged victorious.

The duplicity of Soviet policy was never more evident than in the peaceful stance it maintained toward the United States while encouraging Arab intransigence in the Middle East.

December 7, 1973

Israel voted in a national election on the last day of 1973 and sent the Labor Party back to power but with a reduced margin. It was a foretaste of trends to come.

December 21, 1973

1974

For Israel, 1974 was a year of adjustment to conditions which had been generated by the Yom Kippur War. These included economic problems which were exacerbated by the tremendous cost of the war, amounting to billions of dollars and by the worldwide rise in the price of oil. Inflation, which had been under control for some years, began with the vengeance.

The government, under constant attack for what was deemed to be an error in judgment in not being prepared for the assault on Yom Kippur, appointed a commission under Chief Justice Shimon Agranat to investigate the circumstances of the surprise attack. But it was obvious that those in positions of responsibility would have to pay a political price and in the general elections of December 31, 1973 the ruling Labor coalition lost a number of Knesset seats to the opposition Likud group headed by Menachem Begin. Mrs. Golda Meir, the Prime Minister, was unable to form a majority government and by March had only succeeded in creating a minority group to head the country. She brought Moshe Dayan into the government as Defense Minister but he became the subject of strong attacks by those who had lost sons in the Yom Kippur War and the government fell on April 10th.

In the meantime the Agranat Commission blamed the former Chief of Staff and the Chief of Intelligence for much of what happened. Both were replaced and Mrs. Meir was succeeded by General Yitzhak Rabin, the former ambassador to the United States.

The Israelis arrived at interim truce agreements with both Syria and Egypt. They withdrew from part of the Golan Heights including the city of Kuneitra, the largest community taken by the Israeli army in the 1967 war. A return of prisoners, including 8,000 Egyptians for several hundred Israelis was also made and the eastern bank of the Suez Canal was turned over to Egypt, enabling that country to dredge and reopen the Canal which had been closed since 1967. This was the result of continued shuttle diplomacy of Henry Kissinger whose airline travel must have cost a fortune.

The Arabs, having learned how to flex their oil muscles during the 1973 crisis kept them in good condition throughout 1974. They continued to raise the price of oil while threatening those European states who attempted to furnish that commodity to Israel with a cutoff of supplies. The same threat worked effectively with African and Asian countries and as a result Israel found herself more and more isolated from the international community.

There was combined with this an intensified war of terror fought against Israel by the PLO. The names of towns like Ma'alot, Kiriyat Shemona, Shamir and Bet Shean became internationally famous as the sites of bloody attacks by PLO terrorists against Israeli civilians, more often than not children and schools. The year climaxed with the appearance before the United Nationals of Yassir Arafat who strode down the main aisle of its General Assembly wearing a pistol, and who called for the death of Israel in a speech during which he was constantly interrupted by deafening applause. Shortly thereafter UNESCO refused to admit Israel to any of its meetings or to allow it to participate in programs.

Meanwhile the United States went about the task of repairing its relations with the Arab states and was successful in increasing its influence with Egypt which saw in the Nixon administration its best chance of having the Sinai returned to its jurisdiction. As relations with Egypt improved, those with Israel worsened.

Within Israel the rate of inflation increased as the government was faced with the necessity of paying the bills of the Yom Kippur War. With an inflation rate of 40%, with markets cut off by the Arab threats of oil boycott, and with an economy more and more dependent upon American generosity, the Israelis did not enjoy a very happy year. The full extent of the cost of the war was also brought home when the casualty figures were announced; 2,521 dead and 7,056 wounded, of whom 3,000 were maimed.

Golda Meir resumed her post as Prime Minister but found it more difficult than anyone had expected to form a government. Not until March did she succeed and then only temporarily.

January 4, 1974

February 1, 1974

Meanwhile France, continuing her close relationship with the Arab states, bargained for future oil deliveries by siding against Israel on every issue.

January 18, 1974

Henry Kissinger and his "shuttle diplomacy" brought Israel and Egypt together in an uneasy relationship and negotiated a withdrawal of Israeli forces from the west bank of the Suez Canal.

Israelis feared for the safety of their men taken prisoner by the Syrians during the Yom Kippur War and insisted that a complete list of prisoners and a guarantee of their well-being precede any negotiations on withdrawal from Syrian territory.

February 15, 1974

Israelis worried about the new image of Sadat as a great "peacemaker", bolstered by assistance Egypt received from both the United States and the Soviet Union.

March 1, 1974

While Kissinger proclaimed the necessity for east-west detente, the Soviet Union continued to encourage Arab leaders to take a hard line position regarding peace with Israel.

March 8, 1974

Mrs. Meir found it increasingly difficult to form a government especially when the religious parties failed to agree among themselves on whether or not they should join her coalition.

March 15, 1974

April 5, 1974

Israel celebrated its 26th birthday in an optimistic mood despite all of its travails. However, the terrorist attack at Kiriyat Shemona caused a shadow to be cast over the celebrating.

Many Israelis, worried over the lack of firm leadership at a time when critical decisions had to be made, called for a government of national unity, bringing in all but the Communist and extreme right wing parties.

April 12, 1974

Syrian forces attempted to seize a part of Mount Hermon. Israel took command of the area which afforded a view of the entire Golan and was therefore of great strategic importance. Syrian attacks failed to dislodge the Israelis.

April 19, 1974

Israelis remained suspicious of attempts to downplay their needs in favor of the "larger picture". They saw in many of the moves by the major powers a tendency to bargain away Israel's security in the name of detente.

May 3, 1974

Yitzhak Rabin succeeded Golda Meir as Prime Minister and finally formed a viable coalition without having to call for new national elections.

May 10, 1974

May 17, 1974
The slaughter of 21 high school children in
the Israeli village of Ma'alot set off a wave
of bitterness in Israel against the UN
which had given the PLO tacit and sometimes active support in its terrorist policies.

While the Syrians and their Soviet allies gave every verbal assistance to the PLO, on the Golan Heights they kept a tight rein on Arafat's terrorists. A raid from there might have brought swift retaliation from Israel.

May 31, 1974

June 28, 1974

Meanwhile Arafat continued his international campaign for diplomatic recognition. Buoyed by the ability of the Arabs to wield the oil weapon, the PLO obtained admittance to international conferences and a place on their programs.

A ROSE IS A ROSE IS A ROSE...

IN SAUDI ARABIA

IN EGYPT

IN SYRIA

IN ISRAEL

IN JORDAN

July 5, 1974

President Nixon visited the Middle East in the summer of 1974, issuing placating statements in every capital in which he stayed.

HENRY, THE JUGGLER

As a desperate President Nixon struggled to retain power in the face of the Watergate allegations, Henry Kissinger found himself directing American foreign policy, and trying to deal single-handedly with the ever more troublesome conflicts in the Middle East.

July 12, 1974

July 19, 1974

In the United States also, the question of
whether or not to talk with the heads of
the PLO remained an open issue. It
became even more so after President
Nixon resigned and was succeeded by
Gerald Ford.

July 26, 1974

And the Soviet Union continued to give wholehearted support to the PLO and its Arab supporters.

Throughout the summer of 1974 Israel tried to bring the Arabs to the negotiation table. Every attempt was rejected as the Arabs remained divided in all things except in their hostility to the Jewish state.

August 2, 1974

34

Israelis, paying the fearsome monetary costs of the Yom Kippur War and the resultant oil embargo, found that their pounds were worth less and less. Inflation, long under control, was now climbing steeply upward, a trend that was to accelerate even more in later years.

August 9, 1974

THE CARROT AND THE STICK

August 16, 1974

The Arab states, using the oil weapon, succeeded in persuading every last black African state to sever relations with Israel. In return they gained nothing, not even favorable price reductions in the oil they had to purchase from the Arabs.

35

The UN vote giving the PLO increased status was seen in Israel as another example of blackmail and of posing a greater danger to the prospects of world peace.

August 23, 1974

Archbishop Hilarion Capucci, the Greek Catholic prelate to the west bank and East Jerusalem, was convicted in an Israeli court of smuggling arms and guns to PLO terrorists.

August 30, 1974

Again, as in so many years past, the Arab world and the PLO were permitted to dominate the sessions of the General Assembly, drawing attention away from issues such as the Arab oil blockade, that really threatened the well-being of the small nations of the world.

September 20, 1974

September 27, 1974

Abdul Bouteflika, president of the General Assembly and the Algerian foreign minister, allowed his position to become involved in a partisan issue for the first time when he denounced Israel during his presidency.

November 8, 1974

The bitterness about this in Israel and among her friends elsewhere grew as the hypocrisy in the actions of the United Nations became more and more evident.

In Washington, General George Brown, chief of staff of the United States military, accused American Jews of controlling American banks and access to the American media. His anti-semitic statement was denounced by American political leaders and the General apologized.

November 15, 1974

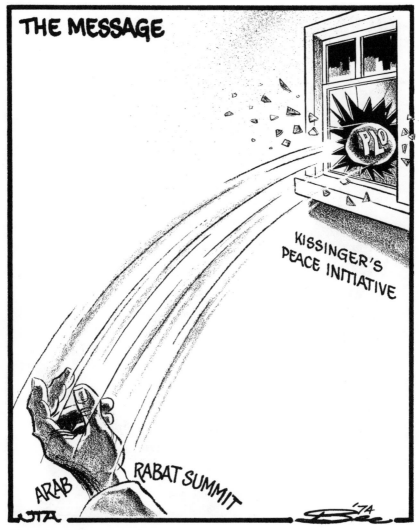

November 1, 1974

At Rabat, Morocco, the Arab leaders met
and stated that the PLO would be the sole
representative of the Palestinian people, a
blow to Kissinger's hopes for peace.

January 10, 1975

Among the United Nations agencies to denounce Israel was UNESCO, with whom Israel had cooperated on many occasions. The move was particularly ill-placed because of the scientific and cultural contributions Israel has made from which all the world benefits.

1975

If 1974 marked Israel's beginning of a recovery from the military, political and economic shocks of 1973 and the Yom Kippur War, 1975 saw the process carried somewhat further — although in some serious respects the year was nothing to be overjoyed about.

It was the year in which the phrase "Zionism equals racism" first gained wide currency. The International Women's Conference meeting in Mexico City adopted it, then the third committee of the United Nations, then UNESCO and the General Assembly of the same organization. Angry American Jews instituted a travel boycott of Mexico after that country supported the Arabs in voting for the resolution but it was almost the only retaliatory measure that could be taken.

Perhaps even more disheartening was the obscene sight of Uganda's Idi Amin receiving a standing ovation in the General Assembly and then deliving a tirade against Jews and Zionism. Only the action of the UN in granting recognition to the Palestine Liberation Organization marked a more unappetizing event. It was not a good year for Israel at the United Nations.

But in another sense the year was a milestone. Even though so noted a personage as Moshe Dayan opposed the decision and there were many questions raised in Israel about its wisdom, the government of Yitzhak Rabin signed the second interim Sinai withdrawal treaty with Egypt, agreeing to return the Abu Rodeis oil fields and the strategic Mitla and Giddi passes in the Sinai. The Suez Canal reopened for business for the first time since 1967 and several ships with cargoes bound for Israel passed through it undisturbed. There were signs of a rapproachement between Israel and Egypt, a greater measure of courtesy between their representatives and a growing estrangement between Egypt and some of the more extreme Arab governments.

Credit for this has to go to the indefatigable Henry Kissinger. Several times during the year it appeared that negotiations might break down and once they were suspended. But shuttle diplomacy won the day and with much patience and a great deal of sitzfleisch Kissinger was able to obtain the signatures he needed to bring the elusive peace he sought just a little bit closer to reality.

To the north, the Lebanese civil war began, rending that country in many parts and destroying its political, social, religious and economic fabric. Israel took some measures to safeguard its northern border and was roundly denounced in the expected quarters for doing so. Within Israel and in other countries the terrorists continued to wreak their havoc; bombs killed many people in Jerusalem, the Savoy Hotel in Tel Aviv was the scene of carnage, and London and Paris were the sites of shootings and explosions as the PLO belied the image of respectability that its friends in the United Nations sought to bestow upon it.

The economic strains of the post-Yom Kippur War period were continuing to make themselves felt. Inflation gradually eroded the value of the Israeli pound, emigration fell off slightly from the high of the previous year but so did immigration, and the general climate of fear led to a more effective anti-Israel economic boycott on the part of Israel's enemies. American firms reduced their commitments in Israel and many openly refused to do business with that country in order to maintain their economic ties with the Arab world. Taxes in Israel rose precipitately and so did many of the manifestations of a society in trouble, crime, drug use, prostitution and other forms of aberrant behavior.

In all, it was a year that Israel could have skipped but neither nations nor people are permitted that luxury. The best that might be said for it is that it could have been a lot worse and, in hindsight we note that the seeds of the coming peace with Egypt were being planted and fed. For that alone it might be regarded as a positive year although — once again — hindsight at some future time may well reverse that judgment.

February 7, 1975
As Israel and the world moved into 1975
the aftereffects of the Yom Kippur War
continued to be felt, especially in the ability of the Arabs to use their oil diplomacy
effectively as blackmail.

DOUBLE SHOT

RIGHT TO EMIGRATE

TRADE TREATY

The Soviet Union, incensed at the American insistence on linking trade with the right of Jews to emigrate, broke off its trade agreement with the United States and drastically reduced the number of Jews permitted to leave.

January 17, 1975

PEACE BY PIECE

SADAT'S SOUVLAKI

TODAY'S SPECIAL! ISRAELI PEACE DOVE ARAB STYLE

Anwar Sadat began making noises about peace with Israel but the conditions he set forth made it difficult for Israelis to take him seriously. Camp David was still some years away.

February 14, 1975

Gradually Arab economic power literally reached into the Western capitals as oil millionaires began buying up land, corporations and other investments. The Soviets stood to gain as the West laid itself open to control by foreigners.

February 21, 1975

Henry Kissinger's shuttle diplomacy produced a second Sinai agreement under which Israel withdrew from the oil fields and the strategic Sinai passes. To some Israelis it appeared that much had been given up, little received in return.

March 28, 1975

THE SENATOR'S RETURN

GREETINGS, FRIENDS AND COUNTRYMEN!

MC GOVERN

PEACE 'AT ANY PRICE' MISSION

JTA

April 4, 1975

Senator George McGovern returned from a visit to Yassir Arafat, proclaiming the justice of a Palestinian state in Palestine and advocating some of the PLO positions. It was a far cry from his election campaign positions of 1972.

GETTING THROUGH TO ARAB 'FRIENDS'

ON ISRAEL

THE PRESSURE

KEEP UP

WE'LL

JTA

In Washington, Israel's friends grew worried over what appeared to be an increasing tendency for American diplomats to side with the oil-rich Arab states and to move correspondingly away from the Israeli position in the conflict.

46

April 25, 1975

April 18, 1975

The Arabs continued to boycott Israel and Jews, thereby providing a classic example of one who cuts off his nose to spite his face. Where would the world be, including the Arabs, were it not for Jewish scientists, doctors and others, including a most impressive list of Nobel Prize winners.

Many American businessmen and the American government refused to acknowledge the legitimacy of the Arab boycott, in sharp contrast to their European counterparts.

May 1, 1975

The Common Market of Europe granted Israel some trading privileges but in general the economic boycott of Israel by the democratic west, excepting the United States, remained in effect.

May 16, 1975

Prime Minister Yitzhak Rabin visited Washington for meetings with President Ford. The pressure applied by the United States on Israel to comply with Arab demands was beyond the point that Jerusalem considered acceptable.

May 30, 1975

The Arab states continued their political and economic support for the Palestinians but refused to bring their ordeal to an end by arriving at a peaceful resolution of the Palestine conflict.

June 6, 1975

August 15, 1975

During the year the number of immigrants to Israel fell and the numbers emigrating tended to rise. The trend alarmed Israelis and Zionists abroad but few solutions were advanced that might change the pattern.

Arab oil pressures and assurances of financial reward won most third world countries to the support of Israel's enemies. It took some years before many of them realized that the Arabs were long on promise and short on delivery.

June 13, 1975

June 27, 1975

Anwar Sadat continued to negotiate with Israel on Sinai withdrawals but his frequent statements of support for the PLO and denunciations of Israeli policy jarred hopes within Israel for an Israel-Egyptian peace.

51

The World Congress of Women met in Mexico and passes a "Zionism equals racism" resolution, in defiance of all common sense and totally out of context with the purposes of the gathering. It was the start of what was to be a world wide campaign.

July 11, 1975

On the one hand Sadat signed agreements with Israel, on the other hand he denounced her at every opportunity. Israelis found it difficult to fathom his true intentions.

August 1, 1975

The Second Sinai agreement with Egypt was signed, thanks again to Henry Kissinger's ability to practice diplomacy on the run. Although many questioned whether or not it would hold, both sides were interested in making it work, and it did.

September 5, 1975

September 12, 1975

King Hussein of Jordan demanded more arms from the United States and threatened to turn to the Soviet Union if they were not forthcoming. The question of American arms supplies to the Arabs bedeviled Israel throughout the year.

53

September 26, 1975

Kissinger spent time traveling to many of the Arab capitals but he found himself stymied by a refusal of the Arab leaders to consider reducing their pressure on the West by compromising on oil supplies and prices.

October 3, 1975

The ugliest sight of the year was that of Idi Amin, slaughterer of hundreds of thousands of his black countrymen, being given a standing ovation by the General Assembly when he came to denounce Zionism and Israel as being racist.

October 24, 1975
The General Assembly finally voted on the
Zionist equals racism issue and passed it,
thereby dredging up old memories of an
Austrian paperhanger who had used
racism for his own purposes a generation
earlier.

November 28, 1975

Daniel Moynihan, America's ambassador to the United Nations, became the best placed spokesman for Israel in the world forum and with a sharp tongue and considerable outspokenness told it to the Arabs "like it was".

The United States remained committed to its pledge not to talk with the PLO as long as Arafat's organization did not recognize Israel's right to exist. But there were frequent reports of quiet meetings behind closed doors, which raised doubts among Israel's supporters in this country.

December 5, 1975

56

1976

July 4th, 1976, was the 200th anniversary of the signing of the Declaration of Independence of the 13 British colonies in North America and American citizens celebrated with fireworks and exhibitions on their bi-centennial day.

But by the close of that day the world had turned its attention away from that celebration to mark another, more contemporary tale of heroism and victory. In the dusk of a Tel Aviv evening there landed at Ben Gurion airport several Israeli aircraft bearing the heroes and the survivors of the Entebbe rescue operation, a courageous and humanitarian act of daring that electrified the world. Not only had Israel's commandos flown into Entebbe airport in Uganda and rescued a planeload of 103 hostages whose lives had been in great danger, they had saved the men and women aboard the Air France jetliner from one of the most cruel and hated despots of modern times, Idi Amin, the butcher of Africa. The cost was the lives of several of the hostages and that of the brave commander of the rescuing forces, Yonatan Netanyahu, but the decisive and surgical manner in which the rescue was carried out was in sharp contrast to the uncertain and fumbling course of action taken by other nations in dealing with terrorist outrages.

Would that the rest of Israel's year matched Entebbe for satisfaction. But it was overall a year in which the fabric of Israeli society seemed to unravel somewhat at the edges. The extent to which Israel's people were disaffected by their government and by conditions in general did not become clear until the general elections of 1977 but the signs were everywhere. At one point in the year an economist estimated that one quarter of the working population was either on strike or threatening to leave its jobs. The aftermath of the Yom Kippur War placed great strains on Israel's economy and on the individual taxpayer and an inflation rate of close to 40% did nothing to make life easier although employment was virtually 100% and tens of thousands of Arabs from the west bank and the Gaza Strip found work in Israeli agriculture and industry.

Two of the most important developments affecting Israel in 1976 took place outside her borders and both were to have long range effects on her political development. In Lebanon the civil war increased in intensity and the Syrian forces which entered the country to try and pacify it remained there under the new guise of an "all-Arab force". To it were added some contingents from neighboring Arab states but the direction of military developments was clearly determined by the Damascus government. However the Arab soldiers kept north of the Litani river and away from Israel's northern border and Jerusalem financed and armed its own force of Lebanese Christians under the leadership of Major Saad Haddad. The "good fence" was opened through which Lebanese Christians living near the Israeli border could come into Israel for work and medical assistance.

In the United States the American people elected Jimmy Carter to the presidency in a campaign in which both Carter and his Republican rival President Gerald Ford, competed in their promises of support for Israel. And Israelis bade a political farewell to a man who had become as familiar to them as their own politicians, Henry Kissinger whose shuttle diplomacy resulted in truce agreements with both Egypt and Syria. Unbeknownst to almost everyone, President Sadat was already sending out the first feelers toward Jerusalem, hints which would lead shortly to his dramatic visit to Jerusalem.

On Friday afternoon, December 10th, Prime Minister Yitzhak Rabin went to Ben Gurion Airport to welcome three F-15 planes being shipped from the United States. The Orthodox United Torah Front took exception to this as a desecration of the Sabbath and brought about a Knesset motion of no-confidence in the government. The National Religious Party, although a part of the governing coalition, abstained from voting and Rabin called for general elections in early 1977. No one could have expected what was to take place on that occasion.

January 2, 1976

As 1976 began, the spectre of the PLO
loomed larger and larger in Israel's life and
in the minds of her friends everywhere.
Backed by Arab oil money and Soviet
diplomacy, the terrorists of Yassir Arafat
seemed to be growing in strength with
every day's headlines.

MEXICAN HAT DANCE

THE OILY ARAB HARMONY BOYS

ECHEVERRIA

ANTI-ZIONIST RESOLUTIONS

A vote by Mexico in support of the United Nations resolution denouncing Zionism as racism brought about a boycott of Mexico by American Jewish tourists and some fancy sidestepping by the Mexican government, explaining away its decision.

January 9, 1976

DANGER SPOTS AHEAD

PLO

LEBANON

WEST BANK

RABIN

PEACE PLANS

GOLAN HEIGHTS

1976 was the last year of the Nixon-Ford era in the White House and Israel's Prime Minister Yitzhak Rabin might be excused if he saw future American-Israeli relations as endangered by a series of pitfalls.

January 16, 1976

60

The civil war in Lebanon mounted in intensity and Israelis watched nervously as their northern neighbor moved toward self-destruction. Moslems and Christians died in increasing numbers as that nation collapsed in an orgy of killing.

January 23, 1976

January 30, 1976

Once again the United States came to Israel's rescue at the United Nations with a veto in the Security Council of of a pro-PLO resolution sponsored by the Soviet Union and its allies.

February 6, 1976

The image of Israel as David, so widely used during the Six Day War of 1967, seemed appropriate once again as the small state, almost completely without oil in its national boundaries, struggled to obtain essential oil elsewhere and also had to contend with the economic clout that oil provided its Arab enemies.

The American Congress engaged in its annual debate over foreign aid, so vital to Israel's survival. But this year the Republican Administration increased the share given to Israel's neighbors by a significant amount.

February 13, 1976

March 5, 1976

Not only foreign aid but permits to purchase military equipment were given to the so-called "moderate" Arab states, including giant C-130 transport planes suitable for bringing troops and heavy equipment to a possible front against Israel.

63

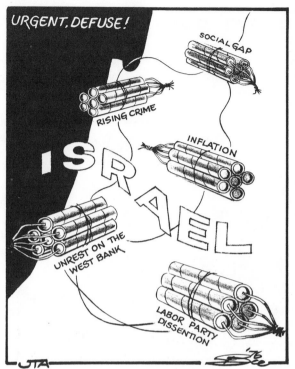

March 11, 1976

The sometimes subtle relationship between Israel's social problems and the West Bank occupation is demonstrated here in a comment that seems a harbinger of events to come a few years later.

In all of the clamor and distraction of current issues, the Jewish people are reminded each year, as spring moves across the world, of the price that was paid for their survival. Yom Hashoa, the Day of Remembrance of the Holocaust, serves that important function.

April 6, 1976

Sadat and Rabin met with and heard from their American allies but, it seemed to many, with strongly different results.

April 16, 1976

May 7, 1976

The Arab boycott, ignored by some, was still effective in the international business community, to Israel's severe economic cost.

LOADING THE WEIGHTS

PRES. FORD

RABIN

HIGH MORALE

550 MILLION

ECONOMIC RECOVERY

JTA

May 14, 1976

The time for American presidential nominations approached and with it the quadriennial debate about American foreign policy. Israel, so dependent upon American economic assistance, watched nervously as President Ford appeared to be withholding support for increased aid.

'BALANCED' REPORTING

Times Daily

ONE ARAB KILLED ON WEST BANK

300 KILLED IN LEBANON

JTA

June 4, 1976

The discrepancy between press coverage of problems on the west bank and those among the Arabs in Lebanon, with the extensive destruction brought on by the latter, raised questions in people's minds about objectivity in journalistic coverage.

July 9, 1976
The picture tells it all: The incredible news
of the rescue of the hostages at Entebbe,
Uganda was received by the entire civilized world with joy and relief.

A FISHY STORY

CHRISTIAN MINORITY

MOSLEM MAJORITY

SYRIA

GREATER SYRIA

Increasingly in Lebanon, control of the country was given over to military forces representing the various warring interests and the Syrians stepped in to "preserve order". Almost lost in the fight for power was its original cause, the struggle of the Christian minority to survive.

July 2, 1976

IT'S TIME TO CRACK'EM!

QADDAFI

AMIN

AFRICA

WORLD OF SANITY & ANTI-TERRORISM

An alliance between Uganda's Idi Amin and Libya's Muammar Khaddafi linked two of the world's most blatant and despicable murderers. They were united in, among other things, their hatred of Israel.

July 23, 1976

American Jews were increasingly worried over the effectiveness of Arab propaganda which they saw proliferating in the lecture halls, the university campuses and in the media. There was an increasing feeling that Israel's cause was being ignored because Arab oil dollars were able to purchase time, space and talent unavailable to Israel and her supporters.

August 20, 1976

September 17, 1976

The annual General Assembly debate on Palestine took place with the predictable arguments, the predictable roll call and the predictable results; nothing was accomplished towards promoting peace in the Middle East.

69

THE NAME OF THE GAME

ELECTION

ISRAEL

JTA

October 8, 1976

Jimmy Carter and Gerald Ford squared off for the 1976 election campaign. Both made expansive promises to Israel's supporters whose votes, they felt, might be decisive in a close election.

NO WAY!

ARAB PROPAGANDA

JUDAISM

JTA

In one area Arab propaganda in the United State failed miserably. It was unable to accomplish a principal objective, the division of the Jewish people in their support for the survival of Israel.

October 29, 1976

Shortly after his defeat by Carter, Ford authorized a vote against Israel in a United Nations debate. The action struck many as contrary to his pre-election commitments to Israel's security.

November 19, 1976

A victorious Jimmy Carter soon learned how the Arabs interpreted his forthcoming presidency; as an opportunity to force the American government to abide by their wishes or face the consequences of Arab anger.

December 19, 1976

January 7, 1977

The most popular TV program of the decade, "Roots", sent American Jews, among others in this country, looking back to their antecedents. For Israel too the lesson was a clear one; its nourishment, its strength came from that source which has always nurtured the Jewish people, the Bible.

1977

As momentous as the shock with which the Yom Kippur began, as full of hope as the arrival of a new baby, as nerve-wracking as a tightrope walker's progress; such was the visit to Jerusalem by Egyptian president Anwar es Sadat in November, 1977. The importance of the visit, and all that it portended for the possibility of peace between Israel and her largest Arab neighbor, overshadowed events that in an ordinary year would have proven overwhelming in themselves.

1977 was the year which saw the ouster of the Labor Party from control of Israel's government, a period that had extended through the entire 29 year history of the state and for several decades before that in Jewish Palestine. Out of the political wilderness where he had languished through one electoral defeat after another came Menachem Begin, former leader of the Irgun Zvai Leumi, a political rival so hated by David Ben Gurion that he would not even say Begin's name in public, a man who was written off for years by the rulers of Israel as a bad joke, a loser, a fanatic, a non-entity. This is the man who won the election of 1977 and who now came to power as Israel's sixth prime minister, the first from outside the ranks of the Labor Party.

Begin's Likud coalition did not so much win the election as the laborites lost it. A series of scandals rocked Israel during the first months of the year. One Labor minister committed suicide, several major personalities were accused of corruption and sent to prison, the prime minister himself, Yitzhak Rabin, was tainted by financial charges and stepped down in favor of Shimon Peres as standard bearer of the party. Tens of thousands of labor votes were siphoned off by the creation of a new party headed by a noted general and archaeologist, Yigael Yadin. People also remembered which party it was that led the nation into the Yom Kippur War debacle and the result was a victory for Begin and his supporters.

In Washington a new president was sending Israel mixed signals. Jimmy Carter, a former governor with no practical foreign policy experience, talked about establishing a homeland for the Palestinians, code words for an independent PLO state on the west bank. He also called for a renewal of peace talks in Geneva, a procedure which would have included the Soviets in the peace process, a move desired by neither Israel or Egypt. Carter sent his secretary of state Cyrus Vance to visit the Middle East but he could accomplish little to diminish the antagonism of the other Arab states towards Israel or to lessen their support for the PLO.

In Lebanon the civil war continued but Israel was not directly involved, continuing her policy of supporting Christian elements situated close to her border. More important, though unknown to the public, were a series of secret talks, in Morocco, Romania and elsewhere, between representatives of President Sadat and those of the Jerusalem government which led to Sadat's historic journey.

Begin was, perhaps, the Israeli most suited to negotiate with Egypt. No one could question his motives regarding the Arabs. The political opposition to such talks within Israel was thus neutralized and when Moshe Dayan deserted the Labor coalition to join Begin's government the Israeli-Egyptian peace talks proceeded without serious hindrance.

With all this Begin pressed forward with a program of creating Jewish settlements on the west bank in opposition to American policy and Egyptian expectations. But those who would point the finger at him should remember that it was the previous Labor government which refused to stand up to the determined settlers and which first equivocated on the issue. At year's end, with talks taking place between Israel and Egypt centering on Sinai, the west bank was pushed into the background by all except the ever-militant, non-compromising PLO. It was a neglect that was to cause serious problems at a later time.

The Israeli election campaign involved several dozen political parties, a few of them of major importance. To the outsider it all seemed an incomprehensible confusion of names, policies, slogans and different interpretations of history.

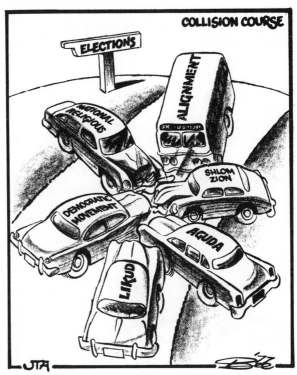

December 31, 1976

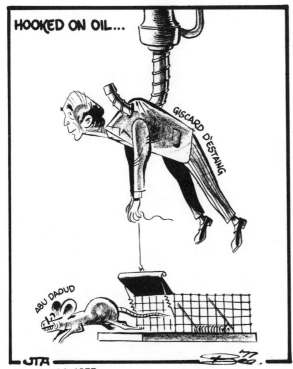

The French government of Giscard D'Estaing earned itself the opprobrium of all civilized countries by releasing the Arab terrorist Abu Daoud because it was afraid of possible retaliation by the PLO if he was tried for murder in a French court.

January 14, 1977

COMING IN ON A WING AND A PRAYER...

OPERATION ORIENTATION

CYRUS VANCE

MIDDLE EAST

Cyrus Vance, the American Secretary of State under the new Carter Administration, traveled to Israel and the Arab states for an orientation session on their varying points of view about the Middle East and American policies.

February 4, 1977

A BUMPY CARPET

ARAB UNITY

POOR VS RICH

LEADERSHIP RIVALRIES

PRO SOVIET~ANTI-SOVIET INFLUENCES

CHRISTIAN~MOSLEM RIFT IN LEBANON

The continuing problem of disunity among the Arab states, which has plagued them ever since the beginning of the Palestine problem, showed no sign of lessening in intensity, even with hatred of Israel as a unifying force.

February 25, 1977

April 1, 1977

Jimmy Carter must have been surprised
to see himself portrayed as a tightrope
dancer but the message was clear; some-
how the new Administration would have to
learn how to keep its balance on the Middle East high wire.

An oft-neglected truth about the PLO was dramatically pictured here. Arafat danced to strings pulled by the Syrian government, a fact especially true because the Syrian presence in Lebanon increasingly restricted the freedom of the PLO to initiate operations against Israel.

March 25, 1977

The world watched with interest as Israelis conducted their national elections. The small country remained one of the few created after World War II to retain its democratic nature despite wars, economic problems and social differences.

April 29, 1977

Terrorism continued to be a principal export of many of the Arab states, especially those who were close to the Soviet Union. There were increasing indications of an international ring of terrorists including Arabs, IRA members, South Americans and others.

May 5, 1977

Sadat was still seen by many as playing both ends against the middle in his dealing with the United States and the Soviet Union. By year's end, of course, this perception was to change drastically.

June 3, 1977

JTA

May 20, 1977

Surprise! To everyone's amazement,
Menachem Begin and his Likud coalition
won the Israeli elections, one of the de-
layed action results of the Yom Kippur War.

It took some time before the extent and significance of the change in Israel's leadership began to register with her friends and her enemies. But within months it was clear that a new hand was at the controls and that many, many things were going to change within and without Israel.

May 27, 1977

In the meantime President Carter carried on negotiations with the various Arab governments, and Israel's friends were afraid that he was about to promise them victories for which Israel would have to pay the price.

June 10, 1977

July 1, 1977

The Arab states also appreciated what seemed to be a change in American policy on Middle East issues; certainly they had little reason to dispute what the Administration was saying or doing on their behalf.

Begin, no baseball fan, looked good as he came to bat for the first time in the international arena.

July 22, 1977

During the summer there were repeated attempts by the United States government to deny that its representatives were meeting with PLO leaders, but to no avail. It appeared obvious that talks of some sort were going on.

August 5, 1977

In Moscow the Soviet Union heated up its anti-Israel propaganda even to the extent of reviving the discredited Protocols of the Elders of Zion, originally fabricated by the Czarist police.

August 12, 1977

The Carter Administration continued to heat up its own campaign, working together with Saudi Arabia to apply pressure on Israel to be more "flexible" on issues such as the future of Jerusalem and of the west bank.

September 23, 1977

Meanwhile the Palestinians, Arabs all, could not find a friendly home in a single one of the Arab countries, who were willing to support terrorism but unwilling to give a place to live to their fellow Arabs.

October 14, 1977

August 26, 1977

As for what the United States was willing to provide for Israel, Menachem Begin saw in it only trouble. The Americans and the Soviets both wanted to carry on Middle East peace talks in Geneva at which the Israelis would be outnumbered and out-maneuvered.

November 18, 1977

The solution to the problem came with
dramatic unexpectedness from Cairo,
where President Sadat was no more willing
to negotiate with the US and the Soviets in
Geneva than were the Israelis. He asked
for and received an audience in Jerusalem
and proposed bi-lateral peace talks, to the
amazement of the world.

November 25, 1977

A stunned world watched as the leaders of
the two great antagonists in the Middle
East wars met and talked together and
agreed to explore the possibilities of peace.

No longer a mirage

ISRAEL

ARAB NATIONS

December 2, 1977

If Sadat accomplished one thing with his trip to Jerusalem, it was to show the rest of the Arab world that peace between Israel and the Arabs was not an impossibility but quite conceivable and even desirable.

It quickly became evident to both east and west that Israel and Egypt were going about the process of creating peace by themselves and shutting both major powers out of the discussions.

December 9, 1977

1978

The euphoria that dominated Israel during the last weeks of 1977 as the result of the November visit to Jerusalem by Egyptian president Anwar es Sadat, dissipated during 1978 like a desert fog before the morning sun. Some of the realities, the contradictions, the conflicts inherent in Israel's problems with the Arab states and with the protagonists in the cold war made themselves evident and threatened for a time to bring the peace process to an ignominious end.

And then, just as it seemed that the entire program was about to collapse, there took place the peace agreement at Camp David in September. But before the concerned parties arrived at that point, there were nervous breakdowns enough to fill a hospital. As follows:

In January the initiative in the peace process passed to the Americans after Sadat and Begin discovered that they could still disagree on basic issues. In Israel second opinions were beginning to be heard about the wisdom of trusting Egyptians to adhere to an agreement. Perhaps, it was said, we would be better off maintaining a state of war than in running the risks of a treaty.

Then in March the PLO struck. Thirty Israelis were massacred on the Haifa-Tel Aviv road and two days later Israeli troops occupied southern Lebanon. The occupation was something less than a success and the PLO forces stationed there escaped to the north.

Within Israel, where inflation and other economic and political problems were much on the minds of the citizens, there was a brief respite from the constant strain of conflict as the result of — of all things — a presidential election. The previous president, Ephraim Katzir, a scientist of international repute, decided to return to his laboratory. In a rare display of unanimity the government and the opposition agreed on Yitzhak Navon to replace him. Navon became the first Sephardi Jew to be elected president of Israel, a largely ceremonial post but with great symbolic importance.

The American government proposed a sale of modern jet fighters to Saudi Arabia and when strong opposition to this was raised in the American congress, tied the proposal together in a package with that of a sale of aircraft to Israel. This began a long period of intense Israeli suspicion of the motives and policies of President Carter. Begin appealed to American Jews to oppose the Saudi sale, a move which was much criticized in the United States as interference by a foreign head of state in domestic politics.

Egyptian attempts to bring other Arab states into the peace process proved futile and a division developed between Cairo and the so-called "moderate" Arab governments that quickly became a chasm. Despite a series of open policy conflicts between Sadat and Begin it quickly became apparent to both of them that if a peace was to be signed it would have to be negotiated primarily by Israelis and Egyptians with the United States acting as an "honest broker" or, at times, the coat holder for both contending parties. Thus no matter how hot the rhetoric got or how far apart the two appeared to be, the substantive negotiating process was never permitted to stop and talks went on in various Israeli and Egyptian meeting places throughout the year. Prominent among the Israelis taking part was a name not new to Jerusalem, where he had been known as a fighter pilot, but which seemed miscast as a diplomat, that of Ezer Weizman. Weizman, who had a reputation as a "flyboy" and a glamorous soldier, proved to be an adept negotiator and established a strong personal friendship with the Egyptian president based upon their mutual military experiences, albeit on opposite sides of the front.

At years end the nation mourned the death of her most famous daughter, one of those who were most responsible for her existence. In a cold rain, thousands walked to the cemetery to bid a sorrowful goodbye to Golda Meir.

December 30, 1977

As the new year dawned Israel and her
friends foresaw a future of peace with her
most powerful enemy. It was to happen,
but not quite as rapidly nor as easily as
people expected.

As with every complex negotiation, each of the interested parties came to the table, or observed from afar, with very different motives and objectives.

January 6, 1978

Yet the talks progressed on many levels. As the negotiators dealt with issue after issue there was growing confidence that they were finally on the road to a settlement of the long and bloody war between Israel and Egypt.

January 20, 1978

The third party in the talks was the United States, acting as the honest broker between the two negotiating nations.

January 27, 1978

February 10, 1978

Israel's supporters sensed an imbalance in the American approach to one of the more sensitive issues affecting her when the Carter Administration began stressing the importance of military support for Egypt.

MISHLOACH MANOT

WARPLANES FOR SAUDIS AND EGYPT

The issue centered around proposed shipments of warplanes to both Egypt and Saudi Arabia, described by the Americans as being "moderate" Arab states.

March 3, 1978

SECURITY BELT

ISRAEL

Talk of peace might be in the air but the PLO was having none of it. Israel strengthened her security measures in the Arab territories under her control.

March 17, 1978

94

As the talks progressed and both sides made proposals and counter-proposals, the suspicion grew in Israel that perhaps Sadat was not willing to go as far as he had earlier indicated.

March 24, 1978

March 31, 1978

Passover served as an occasion to remind the Egyptian president of past rulers of the Nile who had negotiated in less than good faith with the people of Israel.

TIME TO REMEMBER

HOLOCAUST

As ever, Israel's percep-
tions of the world, even
in relatively hopeful
times, were colored by
memories of the
Holocaust.

April 7, 1978

LOOKING FOR A LANDING

HISTORIC RIGHTS

SECURE PEACE

Prime Minister Begin
flew his ship of state to
the United States, trying
to balance two ele-
ments, the need for a
secure and permanent
peace and historic
considerations.

April 14, 1978

April 21, 1978

The 30th anniversary of the founding of
the State of Israel was, for all of the
nation's problems, a hopeful and an
encouraging time. On almost every issue,
security, development, social problems,
there was progress in the working out of
solutions.

April 28, 1978

Meanwhile, back in Washington . . . The
power of the Arab oil countries was felt in
the halls of Congress in the vote on planes
for Saudi Arabia, the largest oil producer
of them all.

And while Saudi Arabia received warplanes from the United States, she was, in turn, doling out huge sums of money to the PLO terrorists.

June 6, 1978

While they, at the same time were slaughtering peaceful Israeli citizens in a series of bloody raids, the worst of them in March, 1978.

June 30, 1978

The opposition leader in Jerusalem, Shimon Peres, of the Labor Party, began a political campaign against Begin, seeking to force new elections for the Knesset.

July 4, 1978

The Soviet authorities tightened their grip on Jews who were demanding the right to emigrate. Many activists were sentenced to long prison terms.

July 7, 1978

In the Knesset the political warfare grew to a pitch that threatened to drown out the more peaceful discussions of the negotiators working toward a Sinai agreement.

July 21, 1978

While acting as though there was no chance for peace, many third world leaders, abetted by the PLO, continued to hurl calumny and hatred at Israel.

August 4, 1978

101

In the United States, President Carter's popularity in the polls slipped badly. His role in the peace talks however continued to reflect favorably upon him and there were many who thought that they might represent his greatest source of political strength.

August 18, 1978

King Hussein of Jordan remained uncommitted during the peace talks, giving ritual support to the PLO but waiting to see what the results would be of the long, drawn out negotiations. The extremist Arab governments, Libya and Syria among them, accused him of selling out to the "Zionist agents."

August 25, 1978

Laboriously, often quietly and out of the spotlight, the committees and the technical experts continued to work on the structure of the peace agreement. It was not a rapid process but it was an effective one.

September 1, 1978

September 8, 1978

The key to it all was the involvement of the United States not only as a friend of both sides but in a practical manner, as the provider of the Sinai Peace Force which was monitoring the existing agreements between Egypt and Israel.

THE CHAMP

At last there was success and the world watched as the three nations announced agreement on a treaty. Both Israel and Egypt gave credit to President Carter for having achieved what long seemed impossible.

September 22, 1978

BRIDGE OVER THE SUEZ

For the first time since 1948 it would be possible for Israelis and Egyptians to visit each other's countries as friends.

September 29, 1978

SKIRTING AROUND

PALESTINIAN STATE

September 29, 1978

The real secret of the agreement was the way in which it skirted a major pitfall, the future of Palestinian aspirations to a state of their own on the west bank of the Jordan river.

October 20, 1978

The agreement was crowned by the news
that both Begin and Sadat were awarded
the Nobel Peace Prize.

But even as the tree of peace was planted, the buzzards flew overhead, looking for ways in which to uproot it when the opportunity might arise.

November 3, 1978

November 10, 1978

Yassir Arafat, frustrated, turned to New York where he might hope to score victories at the United Nations. The world body, under the leadership of Kurt Waldheim, provided him with a forum from which to denounce the Middle East peacemakers.

THE SOWER with strings attached

OIL MONEY

apologies to Millet

JTA

November 17, 1978

On American university campuses and in the board rooms of American industry, the agents of the Arab states, using oil money for their entrance fees, spread propaganda wherever they might influence American leaders against Israel.

THE CORE OF THE MATTER

JERU   SALEM

JTA

December 1, 1978

The problem of the future of Jerusalem, officially regarded by the United States as not a part of Israel, continued to remain a thorn in the relations between Washington and Israel.

December 8, 1978

Goodby Golda!

1979

At the beginning the year the world and the Middle East in particular was shaken by the overthrow of the Shah and the rise of a fanatic Moslem regime in Iran. The new ruler Ayatollah Khomeini pledged his full support to the PLO against Israel.

The high point of the year came early on when, on March 26th the Israeli-Egyptian peace treaty was signed on the lawn of the White House. It was a momentous event witnessed by the whole world, when the two leaders Begin and Sadat on either side of their host President Jimmy Carter, put their signatures to this historic document. One week later Menachem Begin made his first trip to Egypt and was cordially greeted by the people of Cairo.

The signing of the treaty was followed a few days later by Israel's signing an agreement with the United States for the construction of two air bases in the Negev to replace the three bases included in the territory being returned to Egypt. At the end of April the first Israeli ship sailed through the Suez Canal and a month later the Egyptians reoccupied the city of El-Arish in the northern Sinai. President Sadat visited Beersheba and Haifa.

In mid April Israel expressed concern over statements made by some Egyptian ministers that despite the treaty Egypt might participate in hostilities between Israel and other Arabs. But in spite of all the differences there was a lively exchange of official visitors between the two countries. Foremost among them were journeys by Foreign Minister Moshe Dayan, Defense Minister Ezer Weizman and Deputy Premier Yigal Yadin to Egypt and Defense Minister Kamal Hassan Ali and Acting Foreign Minister Bustrus Ghali to Israel.

In the west bank more Jewish settlements were established, in spite of the opposition of the American government. The U.S. administration continued to regard these settlements as illegal and a threat to peace. In Israel there were misgivings about the American support of the Egyptian position in the autonomy negotiations and about U.S. arms supplied to Egypt, Saudi Arabia and a number of other Arab countries. In particular public opinion was disturbed about President Carter's comparison of the Palestinian cause with the civil rights movement in the U.S.A. and the meeting of Ambassador Andrew Young with PLO representatives.

Terrorist attacks by the PLO in northern Israel led to retaliatory actions by Israel in Lebanon but on the whole Israel's good relations with the Christians in southern Lebanon resulted in a relatively quiet year in that area. There was more activity in the west bank where increasing numbers of Jewish settlements led to friction with the Arab population and a noticeable increase in incidents between settlers and Arabs. On September 16th the government lifted a ban on the sale of land in the west bank to private Jewish purchasers. The Supreme Court took the step of prohibiting the purchase of Arab land for the settlers at Elon Moreh on the grounds that it was not needed for security purposes, the reason given for its expropriation. This led to demands by Gush Emunim, representing the Elon Moreh settlers, that the government ease the rules under which land could be obtained for settlers. The conflict was not resolved by the end of the year.

Inflation in 1979 rose sharply, the consumer price index climbing by 114% in the twelve month period. Yet Israelis, whose incomes were indexed to the value of the dollar did not seem to want for much; the stores in Tel Aviv and the apartments in Jerusalem were well furnished. The government reduced subsidies on many essentials.

Differences also developed between Israel and diaspora Jewry on the question of whether or not Soviet Jews should be encouraged to settle elsewhere than in Israel. Growing numbers of them moved to the United States rather than try to make their lives in Israel, a source of bitterness among Israelis that was to grow.

January 5, 1979

The old cliche says that it is always dark-
est just before the dawn. For Middle East
peace watchers, whose dawn was to rise
in just three months, 1979 began with sus-
picions rising in Israel about the sincerity
of Sadat and the ability of President Carter
to withstand Egyptian pressures.

For years Israel had been dependent upon Iran for much of its oil; suddenly this source was denied her as the Ayatollah Khomeini came to power and broke all relations between Israel and Iran.

January 12, 1979

The lack of trust on the part of all of the participants in the Middle East peace process widened the gulf that separated Egypt and Israel, although, below the surface of news bulletins and public statements, the work still went on to create a treaty acceptable to all.

January 19, 1979

113

TRIAL BALLOONS...

Libyans

Palestinians

JTA '79

February 2, 1979

The Americans looked for other means by which Israel and Egypt could be brought together. For a few days there was talk of bringing the Palestinians into the talks and even of involving the Libyans. Neither trial balloon stayed aloft for very long.

What big teeth have you, Grandma!

JTA '79

Meanwhile the Soviet Union, refused access to the peace negotiations, attempted to increase its influence in the Middle East by manipulating the Arab need to market oil, even though the Soviets were themselves oil exporters.

March 9, 1979

114

Sadat's demands were well known; in addition to the Sinai he demanded financial and military assistance from the United States.

March 16, 1979

... and Moses went down the Mount...

The final negotiations on the peace agreement began when Carter invited both leaders to Camp David and virtually locked the door until they worked things out.

March 23, 1979

March 30, 1979

And then, just as all seemed lost, the three men appeared before the television cameras of the world to announce that Israel and Egypt had signed a comprehensive peace agreement.

April 6, 1979

A sense of euphoria permeated the two
nations and it was widely assumed that the
historic breakthrough would lead, inevita-
bly, to additional treaties between Israel
and all but her most implacable enemies.

JAWS

REJECTIONIST FRONT

But it was not to be. The other Arab states, and the Palestinians, refused to recognize the Camp David accord and continued their policies of unremitting opposition to the Jewish State. Egypt was now added to their list of "Zionist agents."

April 13, 1979

STRAUSS' WALTZ

PALESTINIAN AUTONOMY

President Carter designated Robert Strauss to head the American negotiating team in the talks between the Israelis and Egyptians.

May 18, 1979

May 4, 1979

One of the most brutal dictators in the world, Idi Amin, was ousted in Uganda and except for his close ally, Colonel Qaddafi of Libya, few regretted his departure.

May 11, 1979

The people of Israel celebrated "Jerusalem
Day" as they do every year, but with
peace in the air the permanence of a
united Jerusalem seemed more assured
than ever before.

With the rise of an Islamic state in Iran, there was fear that the entire Middle East would be engulfed by fanatic Moslem movements.

May 18, 1979

May 25, 1979

One constant, nagging worry to Israel and her supporters was the growing move on the part of the more radical Arab governments to obtain atomic weapons, a campaign aided by European nations who saw no harm in selling atomic reactors to these unstable governments.

Rebuffed by the United States when the Americans made possible the Camp David agreement, and wooed by the Soviets who purchased oil and offered technological assistance, the Saudis flirted with Moscow but it was a romance that led nowhere.

June 1, 1979

In May Israel returned El-Arish, the principal town in northern Sinai to Egypt. The turnover was a symbolic gesture because only a very small number of Israelis had settled in that area.

June 6, 1979

It soon became obvious that the stumbling block to further development of the peace treaty would not be in the Sinai but in the west bank and the Gaza Strip. Here negotiations for autonomy broke down over different interpretations and the refusal of the Palestinians and the Jordanians to participate.

June 15, 1979

June 22, 1979

In Teheran the religious extremists of the Ayatollah Khomeini began a persecution of the Jews of Iran, condemning some to death on charges of Zionist subversion and imprisoning many others.

A TIGHT SQUEEZE

As the United States and the Soviets held talks about Salt II, difficulties grew for the Soviet Jews desiring to emigrate.

RIGHT TO EMIGRATE

July 6, 1979

HIGHWAY ROBBERS

OPEC

USA

The price of OPEC oil continued to rise and the United States found its sources of energy becoming too expensive to allow it to maintain its spendthrift habits. The effect on the American economy, was direct and damaging.

July 19, 1979

July 5, 1979

Representatives from Egypt and Israel
continued to meet in discussions on the
autonomy of the west bank but the more
they talked the more intractable the problem seemed to be.

July 20, 1979

If there existed one beneficiary from OPEC's continued price rises it was the Soviet Union, which saw its vast oil reserves increase in value while at the same time watching the economic chaos that the price of energy was causing the western powers.

Austrian Chancellor Bruno Kreisky, a Jew who lived through the Holocaust, was the first west European head of state to offer official recognition to Yassir Arafat and the PLO.

July 27, 1979

The Soviets, the Khomeini regime in Iran and the Arab radicals such as Libya and Syria, did what they could to undermine the stability, shaky at best, of the Saudi Arabian royal family.

August 2, 1979

127

ARABESQUE

OIL

OIL

EUROPE

JTA

August 17, 1979

Yassir Arafat continued his attempts to obtain recognition from the nations of the world, traveling from one capital and one meeting to another.

ROGUES' GALLERY

—That's the good guy!

MODERATE   EXTREMIST

$1600 $1600

ARAFAT YASSIR
Age 50
Weight
Heig

JTA

August 31, 1979

There were signs that Carter saw in Arafat a moderate leader rather than a terrorist responsible for countless acts of terror.

August 24, 1979

Willy Brandt of West Germany and Bruno Kreisky of Austria, both members of the Socialist International joined in recognizing Arafat and the PLO as representatives of the Palestinian people.

August 17, 1979

President Carter, in a statement, equated
the Palestinians with the American civil rights
movement, a thought that drew immediate
condemnation from many quarters.

The Israeli government attempted to loosen economic controls and establish a free economy in order to harness the runaway inflation.

September 14, 1979

September 21, 1979

Andrew Young, the U.S. Ambassador to the United Nations, after being fired by Carter for admitting that he had met with a PLO representative, took some verbal shots at Israel.

Yehuda Blum, Israel's new ambassador to the United Nations, may not have felt like Daniel in the lion's den but the parallel was easily suggested because of the huge anti-Israel majorities regularly mobilized by the "third world" countries in the General Assembly.

October 26, 1979

In Jerusalem, Israel's policy on west bank settlements and Arab autonomy led to opposition from Begin's foreign minister Moshe Dayan, who felt that increased autonomy for the Arab populations was desirable. That resulted in Dayan's resignation.

November 16, 1979

The American media
continued its negative
reporting, picturing
Israel, and especially the
Begin government in a
bad light.

November 22, 1979

Minister of Finance
Yigal Hurwitz took over
direction of Israel's
economy and instituted
major changes in policy
aiming at curbing the
steadily increasing inflation and at improve-
ment of the balance
of trade.

December 21, 1979

133

President Carter's foreign policy advisor, Zbigniew Brzezinski, on his visit to North Africa made an unofficial contact with Arafat.

November 23, 1979

At year's end the "unholy trio" of Khomeini, Qaddafi and Arafat still worked closely together, coordinating policies, terrorist training and campaigns against Israel and the western democracies.

December 28, 1979

134

1980

For Israel, 1980 was a year of turmoil and uncertainty. Two of her best known political and military leaders resigned from the cabinet and in the United States, center of Israel's external support, things seemed to stand still as the Americans took part in their quadrennial political exercise. The west bank pot simmered and at times threatened to overflow, and within the country the economic picture continued to darken. Only one area gave hope that things might be better on the morrow; the peace treaty with Egypt was working well and steps to implement it were taken even ahead of its complicated scheduling.

It was the year of the hostage crisis and of the beginning of the Iran-Iraq war, with all that both events meant for continued Middle East instability. The first of these dominated American attention and diplomacy, the second polarized the Arab world around an issue that had very little to do with Israel.

The Soviet invasion of Afghanistan coupled with the Iraqi assault on Iran and the continued detention of American hostages, led President Carter to set up a series of joint military exercises with Egypt. Israelis felt that their country offered the United States a more reliable and stronger ally but political considerations brought the Americans to Cairo instead of to Jerusalem. The lesson was instructive to Israel; the focus of Mid-East attention had shifted away from her and from the Palestine issue to the greater crisis of the Persian Gulf and she and her problems were regarded as somewhat superfluous.

A series of meetings between Israeli and Egyptian leaders, aided in no small part by Sol Linowitz, President Carter's aide on the peace treaty, saw the western two thirds of the Sinai returned to Egypt by the end of January and the borders between the two countries opened for tourism and trade. Envoys were exchanged and both countries determined to arrive at an agreement on west bank autonomy by May 26th. The negotiations continued with the visible differences of approval, as to the ultimate solution to the Palestinian problem.

A meeting between Sadat and Begin in Aswan in January failed to produce a satisfactory agreement on autonomy and the Egyptians refused even to discuss an Israeli plan for the future of the west bank and Gaza which the Egyptians claimed was not in accord with the Camp David agreement. In February the Israeli cabinet approved in principle the right of Jews to settle in Hebron, largest of the west bank cities. The United States disapproved strongly. In May PLO terrorists murdered six Israelis returning from Shabbat prayer in Hebron and later Jewish terrorists seriously wounded two Arab mayors by planting bombs in their automobiles. PLO terrorists attacked Kibbutz Mizgav Am in northern Israel and Israeli army units advanced into Lebanon to wipe out PLO bases in the area.

Several west bank Arab mayors were deported by the Israeli government, a move which led to serious unrest in the territory. The Israelis pointed out that in free elections conducted in the west bank, PLO supporters had won a majority of the posts, a situation which grew more intolerable as conditions worsened.

During the crisis Israeli's defense minister, Ezer Weizman, a former air force chief, resigned in protest over aspects of west bank policies and his post was taken by Begin. Foreign Minister Moshe Dayan also resigned over differences on the west bank and was replaced by Yitzhak Shamir.

President Carter lost his fight for reelection and Ronald Reagan prepared to move into the White House. Israel hoped that a Republican administration might be more accommodating to her needs. Looking to the future, after a year which saw the European Community issue a statement in support of the PLO by America's allies, Israel felt that the change, in many ways, might be for the best.

There was no lessening of the destruction caused by terrorists from many countries, representing many causes, as the new year began. There were renewed charges, backed by evidence, that the various terrorist groups were working more closely together, aided by Libya and some of the Soviet bloc countries.

January 4, 1980

January 17, 1980

The Ayatollah Khomeini, having welcomed the PLO into Iran and given it Israel's embassy in Teheran, seemed, in the American hostage crisis, to have learned some of its more infamous tactics.

137

Khomeini and his fellow Moslem extremists, although professing a hatred for Communism, found no difficulty in aligning themselves with the Soviets in an anti-Israel coalition.

January 25, 1980

Even the Saudis, whose religious extremism is tempered by their vast oil wealth, refused to acknowledge the dangers inherent in Soviet policy and persisted in claiming Israel as their most immediate source of peril.

February 29, 1980

Despite all this the United States continued to sell vast quantities of arms to the "moderate" Arab states over the objections of Jerusalem which felt that the true target for this advance equipment was Israel.

March 7, 1980

The European Economic Commission was contemplating recognizing the PLO as the representatives of the Palestinians, another success in Arafat's campaign to change the image of the terrorist group to a diplomatic entity.

April 11, 1980

139

March 27, 1980

The Carter Administration vacillated
between support for and opposition to
Israel's policies in her dealings with the
PLO and with the large anti-Israel, anti-
Zionist majority in the United Nations.

Yigal Allon (the name means "oak" in Hebrew), commander of the Palmach during Israel's War of Independence in 1948, and author of the "Allon Plan" for the disposition of the west bank, died in March.

March 28, 1980

Once again Prime Minister Begin and President Sadat visited Washington, separately this time, and the receptions they received were decidedly different in nature.

April 8, 1980

May 8, 1980

Ezer Weizman, Israel's
dynamic Minister of
Defense, resigned from
the government be-
cause of differences
with Begin on the ques-
tion of how to carry out
the Camp David agree-
ments on the future of
the west bank.

Camp David had
assumed that both the
Palestinians and Jordan
would join the negotia-
tions on the future of
the west bank. Both
refused, and nothing the
Israelis or the Egyptians
could say would induce
them to change their
minds.

May 9, 1980

Meanwhile pressure on Israel continued from the White House to accede to Palestinian demands to a homeland on the west bank and the Gaza Strip. Again it seemed as though the Jewish state was being traded off for oil interests.

May 23, 1980

In the United States it was presidential election time once again and every hopeful sang the same tune when it came to wooing the Jewish vote, concentrated as it is in the major states with the greatest number of electoral votes.

May 30, 1980

WAITING FOR THEIR TURN

FRANCE

W. GERMANY

ISRAEL

BRITAIN

June 6, 1980

The campaign in western Europe to discredit Israel was kicked off by the British foreign secretary Lord Carrington, who kept pressuring the Jewish State to come to an agreement with the terrorists.

OIL POWER IS PEACE...! PEACE MEANS END OF ISRAEL ... WE WANT WHOLE OF PALESTINE...

Propaganda **R**esponse

ISRAEL'S SIDE OF THE STORY

The Arab propaganda campaign grew steadily in intensity and became more sophisticated while Israel stuck to its outmoded ways of "hasbarah" (explanation).

June 27, 1980

144

July 11, 1980

The European Community, meeting in Venice, extended recognition to the PLO as the legitimate representatives of the Palestinian Arabs. It did not require much thinking to understand why that decision was made.

July 17, 1980

One of the aspects of the PLO's newfound respectability that most infuriated the Israelis was the willingness of the European states to forgive and forget the long record of murder and terror compiled by the PLO in those very same countries.

Jerusalem, facing up to economic realities, announced a reduction in its defense budget, in sharp contrast to those of its neighbors.

July 25, 1980

August 1, 1980

British Foreign Minister Lord Carrington spoke in the United Nations and elsewhere in support of recognition of the PLO, and drew a sharp response from Prime Minister Begin.

August 4, 1980

Once again the Arabs, utilizing their automatic majority in the General Assembly, achieved a condemnation of Israel. It was an annual event, made meaningless by the fact that the Assembly never seemed to find the time or the interest to deal with problems of a more critical and immediate nature.

One of the more distressing elements of the new acceptance of the PLO was the ease with which meanings were reversed; it was as if by changing the meaning of words one could change the bloody history and make acceptable the unspeakable goals of terrorism.

August 8, 1980

U.N. OLYMPICS 1980

NEW ANTISEMITISM

General Assembly Resolution

JTA

August 29, 1980

In Moscow the 1980 Olympic Games were taking place while in New York the United Nations appeared to be engaged in a contest of its own, albeit a more destructive one.

...BEYOND THE CALL OF DUTY

Even the United Nations Secretariat, headed by Austria's Kurt Waldheim, appeared to join in the attacks on Israel by giving support to the PLO's campaign in the UN.

September 15, 1980

MASTER BUILDERS

Libya's Colonel Khaddafi and Syria's President Assad announced that they were uniting into one Arab state. Their governments and armies would merge. It was a pledge heard often before in the Arab world and like those before it, came to nothing.

150

October 3, 1980

For once one could
observe a war which
both sides ought to lose.
When Iraq invaded Iran,
Israel cheered both on
to defeat. Never had
one enemy so thoroughly
deserved another.

October 24, 1980

Soon it was the turn of
French president Giscard
d'Estaing to come out in
support of the PLO.

October 31, 1980

151

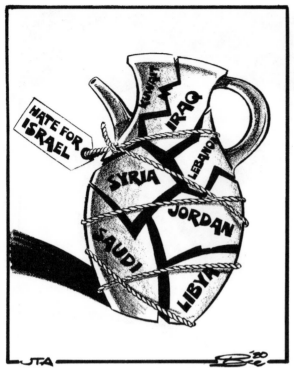

Egypt excepted, the Arab nations were never more at odds with each other and rarely more unified in their condemnation of Israel. It appeared to be the only issue on which they could get together without firing guns at each other.

December 12, 1980

Carter lost the American election; Ezer Weizman, who had stirred up a storm of controversy by urging American Jews to vote for him, was out of the Likud party.

December 19, 1980

December 26, 1980

With a Republican Administration in power, Senator Charles Percy of Illinois became chairman of the Senate Foreign Relations Committee. Suddenly he too was discovering the virtues of Yassir Arafat. It was not a good way for Israel to end the year.

1981

The year 1981 began with two events which affected Israel strongly although at the time it was difficult to assess the extent to which she would be influenced by them. The first was the inauguration of a new American president, a Republican who was widely viewed as the best friend Israel had had in the White House in 20 years. The second, occurring on the same day, was the end of the 444 day American hostage drama.

With the Egyptian peace treaty signed and in effect, Israel's principal concern during 1981 had to do with the Palestinians rather than, as had heretofore been the case, a possible outbreak of warfare with the countries on her borders. None of them was strong enough to engage Israel in conflict without Egyptian support. A siege of shelling of Israel's northern settlements by PLO units in Lebanon brought a statement from Egyptian president Sadat to the effect that while he supported the idea of a Palestinian government in exile, should it be formed, he opposed a leading role in such a government for the PLO. The situation in Lebanon deteriorated to the point where Israel warned Syria that she would not stand by if Christian forces in that country were threatened by the Syrian army.

At the end of April Israel shot down two Syrian helicopters and the next day the Syrians began installing Soviet made SAM 6 missile bases in the Bekaa Valley in eastern Lebanon. The Israelis threatened to destroy the Syrian missile bases and war was averted by the American special envoy Philip Habib who arranged a compromise; the missiles would be untouched but there would be a cessation of raids and rocket attacks across Israel's northern frontier.

This compromise was easier for the Syrians and PLO to agree to after a dramatic demonstration of Israeli technological and military capability in June. On the sixth of that month the Israeli air force destroyed the Iraqui nuclear reactor near

Baghdad. The Israelis claimed that the reactor was intended to build atomic bombs for use against Israel, a goal the Iraquis had never seriously refuted. The American government reacted by temporarily suspending further shipments of military aircraft to Israel but these were resumed later.

Within Israel elections were held and, after an impassioned campaign which saw the Labor Party unable to unite under a single leader, Begin was re-elected although his coalition was recreated with the narrowest of majorities. Only the support of the religious parties enabled him to remain in power and as a part of the price he paid for bringing them into the coalition, he agreed to amend the Law of Return so as to exclude Jews converted by Conservative or Reform rabbis. A bitter reaction from non-Orthodox Jews in the diaspora forced the government to back down but other measures tightened the hold of the religious elements within Israel.

In October the world was stunned by the assassination, by Moslem religious fanatics, of President Sadat of Egypt. He was succeeded by vice president Hosni Mubarrak in a smooth transition of power. Mubarrak pledged to carry out the terms of the Camp David treaty which assured Egypt of a return of the eastern third of the Sinai in April, 1982.

Israel and its American allies suffered a serious political blow when the United States Senate voted to sell Saudi Arabia AWACS air defense equipment after a bitter struggle that both sides agreed marked a turning point in Israel's relations with the United States. For the first time Israel's supporters lost a Congressional decision on which they had staked their prestige and into which they had thrown their every resource. It did not bode well for future encounters with the Reagan Administration.

Moshe Dayan died in the latter part of the year and Israel mourned the passing of one of her most famous sons. Then, during the final week of the year the Israeli government placed the Golan Heights under civilian rule, tantamount to annexation. It was an act which seemed to signal a new and harder policy toward her Arab neighbors.

February 6, 1981

Prime Minister Begin no sooner watched
the new year come in than he saw his
governing coalition disappear. For a while
he ruled with a minority but it soon
became apparent that new elections were
going to take place.

In Saudi Arabia King Khalad called for a Jihad a Moslem holy war against the Jewish State.

February 13, 1981

February 20, 1981

The West German government began the sale of tanks to Saudi Arabia. The question of why the Saudis might need such modern equipment was overshadowed by the fact that it was Germany who chose to help arm one of Israel's most implacable enemies.

157

DAY OF A SALESMAN

EUROPE

CAMP DAVID

EUROPEAN INITIATIVE

JTA

February 27, 1981

Egyptian President Sadat traveled to Europe to bolster his sagging economy and to strengthen his hand in the autonomy negotiations with Israel.

IN REVERSE AND DOWNHILL

PLO

CAMP DAVID

JTA

In so doing he seemed at times to be returning to his former supportive position regarding the PLO. It was an uncomfortable sight for those who had signed a peace treaty with Egypt.

March 6, 1981

In Washington the new Administration had its hands full with economic and political problems. Camp David was lower on its list of priorities.

March 20, 1981

THE DESERTER

DIASPORA

Israel was faced with the problem of how to deal with a growing rate of emigration. This posed a major moral as well as a practical crisis for the Jewish State.

March 27, 1981

THREE IS A CROWD

In the pre-election campaigning in Israel, Moshe Dayan suddenly entered the lists with his own following, causing problems for both Begin and Labor Party leader Shimon Peres.

May 1, 1981

"Those who ignore the lessons of history ......" (SANTAYANA)

SALE OF MILITARY EQUIPMENT TO THE SHAH

SALE OF AWACS TO THE SAUDIS

The Republican Administration proposed to sell to Saudi Arabia AWACS reconaissance aircraft and equipment. This took place a couple of years after vast quantities of American equipment fell into the hands of Moslem extremists who overthrew the Shah of Iran.

May 8, 1981

In Libya, Colonel Khaddafi continued his romance with the Soviet Union despite his ideological distaste for its political and anti-religious philosophy.

May 15, 1981

In West Germany, Schmidt continued his wooing of the Arab states and extended a helping diplomatic hand to the PLO and Yassir Arafat.

May 22, 1981

June 5, 1981

But all of the attempts by the Arabs, armed with their oil wealth, to put an end to the existence of Israel, failed on the rock of Israel's moral, military and political strength.

King Hussein of Jordan, odd man out in the political maneuvering that surrounded the Palestine problem, began receiving support from an unexpected source, the Soviet Union.

June 12, 1981

HOME ON THE RANCH...

June 19, 1981

The Israelis looked across the Lebanese border and saw PLO camps, Syrian missiles and serious military threats. But the Americans, with Philip Habib as negotiator, dissuaded them from moving into Lebanon to finish off their enemies.

July 3, 1981

The Israeli destruction of the Iraqui
nuclear reactor blew apart Baghdad's
hopes of destroying Israel once its bombs
were operational.

July 24, 1981

The Israeli elections ended inconclusively
but the real winners were the religious parties who held the balance of power and
negotiated for a high price.

Let's put it together again!

ASHKENAZIM SEPHARDIM

JTA

July 31, 1981

One aspect of the election that dismayed all observers was the tendency to identify voters and parties by ethnic origin, adding to the social divisions already operating among the Jews of Israel.

JUST A FRIENDLY PUSH

RESTRAINT AGAINST PLO

HABIB

JTA

August 21, 1981

Philip Habib's negotiating powers were viewed somewhat ruefully in Jerusalem but in the end they proved to be too powerful to contest and the Israelis agreed not to take out the Syrian missile bases in Lebanon.

August 7, 1981

The decision of Israel to bomb PLO positions in Southern Lebanon was aimed at discouraging terrorist incursions and rocket attacks against the Jewish State.

Once again the world became aware of the international nature of terrorism and of the Soviet influence in its development and operations.

August 14, 1981

THE HOSTAGES

Despite the agreement on Lebanon, Israelis felt that the PLO was using the Lebanese as hostages to Israeli behavior, much as the Iranians had done with their American hostages the year previous.

August 28, 1981

Anwar Sadat took up the cudgels for the PLO, claiming that without a Palestinian state on the west bank justice would not be served. The Israeli government looked somewhat askance at its new partner in peace.

THE GREAT PROMOTER

September 4, 1981

NOTHING CAN STAND IN THE WAY OF OUR FRIENDSHIP!

KREISKY

VIENNA SYNAGOGUE VICTIMS

October 2, 1981

In Vienna Arab terrorists interrupted a Bar Mitzvah ceremony with bombs, killing several worshippers. It was in the land of the Jewish premier Kreisky who had been the first western European head of state to extend recognition to the PLO.

169

September 18, 1981

The AWAC debate in the U.S. Congress
hung heavily over Israel with the Administration staking all its prestige on the proposed sale to the Saudis.

Once again, as in every Autumn, the United Nations met to pass its annual anti-Israel resolution at the behest of the PLO and its Moslem and Soviet allies.

October 9, 1981

The Reagan Administration, still professing support for Israel, but intent on providing Saudi Arabia with military equipment far beyond its needs, proved an enigma to Israel's policy planners.

October 16, 1981

October 30, 1981

The AWACS vote, into which Israel and
its American friends had poured so much
commitment and effort, seemed, at its los-
ing, to paint Israel into an impossible
corner. Worse, it presaged a series of such
Senate defeats in battles to come.

November 6, 1981

Anwar Sadat died in October under a hail
of assassins, bullets, mourned by his people and his ancient foes, now friends.

U.S. MISGUIDED MISSILE

No sooner did Saudi Arabia get the AWACS than it also received Richard Nixon, traveling there on business after he supported the Saudi position on AWACS.

November 13, 1981

CARRYING THE WRONG BAG

President Reagan made a remark about foreign influence on American decisions which was clearly a swipe at Israel's American supporters on AWACS. The truth was that the Saudi government was much more active in influencing American lawmakers than Israel could ever hope to be with her far more limited financial resources.

November 20, 1981

December 4, 1981

Moshe Dayan, an iconoclast to the end,
finally succumbed to cancer after a battle
of many years.

The Saudis came up with an eight point Palestinian peace plan which did not even refer to Arab recognition of the right of Israel to exist as an independent state. The Americans appeared interested; the other Arabs sank it because it was too "moderate."

November 27, 1981

Meanwhile the Americans seemed to be veering towards a Middle East policy based on support for the Saudi and Jordanian kingdoms.

December 11, 1981

Bitterness grew between Israel and American Jews over the fact that more and more Soviet Jews chose to come to this country in preference to Israel, which had managed to secure their exit permits from Russia.

December 18, 1981

unpublished

As the year drew toward its end Israelis felt more and more restricted in their freedom of action by American insistence that they not move in Lebanon while Washington continued to give military and political support to their enemies.

177

CHARLIE MC KLUTZNICK

In New York Philip Klutznick, a leading Jewish layman, suggested that the Saudi "peace plan" was worth a second look. In this he stood virtually alone in the Jewish world.

L.A. Messenger — December 18, 1981

STRATEGIC WRAPUP

MEDICAL SUPPLIES BY REAGAN & REAGAN

The newly signed strategic agreement between Israel and the United States was of a very limited nature and offered Israel very little.

December 25, 1981

178

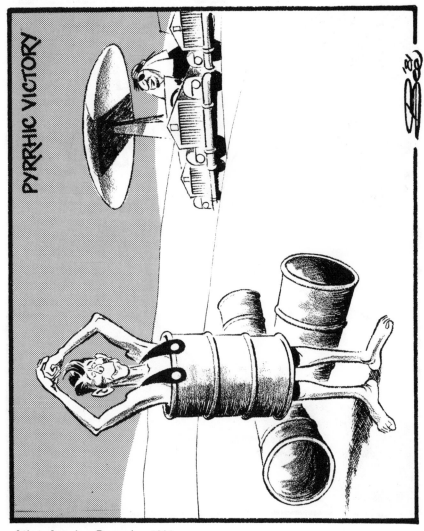

Life in Israel — December 1981

The AWACS victory of the Administration over Israel's supporters began to look less admirable as the Saudis made it more and more evident that they did not see the AWACS deal as anything more than a commercial transaction; they owed the Americans nothing in return for the valuable equipment about to be placed at their disposal.

January 1, 1982

The annexation of the Golan Heights at
the end of the year signaled a new and
more intransigient Israeli policy towards
those who refused to come to the peace
table with them.

1982

Year 1982 will go down in Middle East history in which peace came at last to one of Israel's troubled borders, that with Egypt, and war erupted with a significance not yet evident, on another, that with Lebanon.

The final third of the Sinai desert was returned to Egyptian control by the Israelis on April 25th but not before Israel underwent a traumatic experience that threatened for a time to upset the carefully planned procedure by which a conflict that had lasted for 34 years and cost thousands of lives was finally ended.

The final evacuation of Yamit took place amidst the forcible removal of Jewish diehards and the blowing up of every building in the town by the Israeli army and police. As the Israeli flag was lowered and the Egyptian flag raised after 15 years of occupation, the Egyptian government called on other Arab states to follow in its footsteps and negotiate peace with Israel.

Less than two months later, on June 4th, a PLO agent attempted to assassinate the Israeli Ambassador to London, Shmuel Argov. Though grievously wounded, he survived, but what did not survive was Israel's fragile truce with Lebanon, Syria and the PLO. That had lasted for ten months during which time Israel's northern border remained quiet.

On June 6th Israel launched **Operation Peace For Galilee**, whose goals were originally described by the government as being the clearing of a strip of 40 kilometers in southern Lebanon of any vestige of PLO operations, in order to secure the northern population of Israel from fear of terrorist attack. Within a few days it was clear that the Israelis were not confining their military operation to this confined area but were moving against the PLO in all of Lebanon south of Beirut.

Sidestepping the Syrian army positions in the Bekaa valley, the Israeli contingents moved into the southern suburbs of the Lebanese capital, uncovering vast caches of PLO military stores and destroying the elaborate PLO military and quasi-civilian administrative structures that had made much of southern Lebanon occupied territory.

In the process the Israelis were able to contain the Syrian air force and destroy the Syrian missile positions in Lebanon which had seemed so threatening when they were first installed in 1981. No single Arab country, including Syria, offered substantial military assistance to the PLO during its struggle with Israel.

The Israelis began a seige of west Beirut, where the Moslem population lived, with the intention of forcing the evacuation of the PLO terrorists holed up in its Palestinian camps and other centers. After repeated Israeli bombings and with the cooperation of Syria and the moderate Arab states an evacuation plan was devised and Arafat and thousands of his men left Beirut for exile in several Arab countries.

Shortly afterwards the leader of the Maronite Christian population, Bashir Gemayel was elected president and then, a few days later, assassinated by Moslem enemies. The Israeli army, which had evacuated its positions in west Beirut, reentered the city in order to protect the civilian population but was unable to prevent a massacre of Palestinians living in two refugee camps, by Maronite Christian forces.

The world reacted strongly to these killings, which were viewed on TV screens in every country, and demanded an investigation. At first the Israeli government refused but then bowed to pressure, much of it from within the country.

At years end the investigation was concluding its hearings into the extent to which Israeli government officials and military officers knew of the killings while they were taking place. At the same time US sponsored talks between Israel and Lebanon were hopefully leading toward evacuation of that country by all foreign forces and the signing of a peace treaty between the two nations.

January 8, 1982

The Soviet Union destroyed the Polish
Solidarity worker's movement and there
were those who compared the move with
the willingness of the American government to sell arms to the enemies of her
ally Israel.

January 15, 1982

One of the reasons of course was the continued flow of American dollars and other western currencies to the Arab states in return for their single asset, oil.

In Jerusalem a worried goverment counted the days until April when the final third of the Sinai desert was scheduled to be returned to Egypt.

January 22, 1982

It seemed to some that the Reagan Administration was deliberately testing the resistance of the Israel government in its growing tendency to provide greater military support for the "moderate" Arab governments.

February 5, 1982

February 12, 1982

President Mubarrak invited Soviet industrial experts to help the Egyptian economy.

It was Weinberger who insisted that the AWACS planes would be used to safeguard Saudi Arabia's Persian Gulf frontier but the Saudis themselves insisted that Israel, not the Soviet Union or even Iran was their primary enemy.

February 19, 1982

SPRING CLEANING

WEST BANK

PLO PLO PLO PLO

On the west bank a series of riots and disturbances broke out, causing casualties on both sides and strengthening the hold of the Israeli army on the cities and villages of the region.

March 19, 1982

186

CUISINE A'LA MITTERAND

RENEWED FRANCO-ISRAELI FRIENDSHIP

April 9, 1982

French President Francois Mitterand's
visit to Israel was a welcome relief in its
warmth and open nature. Mitterand, a
Socialist, had a long record of friendship
with the Jewish state.

What will the future bring?

April 2, 1982,

With the scheduled withdrawal from Sinai ten days off, all eyes were on Egyptian President Mubarrak for signs of how or if Egyptian policy towards Israel might change after the return of territory.

How goodly are your tents, O Jacob...

FALASHA JEW

The black Jews of Ethiopia, struggled to escape persecution by that country's new pro Soviet rulers. But they found a poor response in Jerusalem to their pleas for rescue.

April 16, 1982

One indication of how things would go was the announced intention of the Egyptian government to maintain its good relations with Israel while trying to establish a rapprochement with the other Arab states.

April 23, 1982

The Israeli government instituted civilian rule on the west bank in hopes of improved cooperation for autonomy from the local Arab population.

April 30, 1982

PRICE OF PEACE

May 5, 1982

The fateful day came and went, the Israelis
left and the Egyptians took over and the
world did not come to an end. It was a
hopeful beginning to a new era on the history of the troubled part of the world.

Operation "Peace for Galilee"

Life in Israel—summer issue, 1982

The Israeli move into Lebanon came as a blessed relief to Christian Lebanese who had been living under the thumb of the PLO terrorists in southern Lebanon.

AFTER THE AMPUTATION

JTA

June 25, 1982

The reputation and stature of PLO leader Yassir Arafat took a severe beating even as his forces in Lebanon suffered a complete defeat on the field of battle.

For Israelis in the northern part of the country the end of the threat of PLO attacks meant the first peaceful summer in years.

July 2, 1982

July 9, 1982

For many in Israel General Ariel Sharon was the hero of the campaign. They saw him as an effective leader against the nation's enemies.

As Beirut was besieged hopelessly, the PLO forces had no place to go. No Arab countries were eager to provide refuge for its terrorists.

July 16, 1982

Further to the east Iranian soldiers moved into Iraq. The silence that enveloped that war was deafening, especially in the halls of the United Nations.

194

July 30, 1982

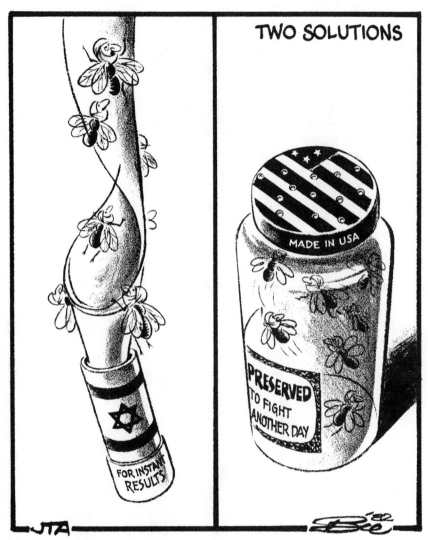

August 13, 1982

Surprised at the swift advance of the
Israeli forces, the U.S. Government
favored the evacuation of the PLO forces
from Lebanon intact.

Bombings of Jewish buildings in France and other anti-semitic outbreaks in Europe increased as the Israelis continued their siege of Beirut.

August 20, 1982

The opposition Labor party launched a campaign to bring King Hussein into the peace process.

August 27, 1982

Arafat, rescued from Beirut by American intervention, proclaimed victory in the Lebanese fighting. It was a hollow boast.

September 3, 1982

September 10, 1982

The invasion of Lebanon brought out of the woodwork all the elements hostile towards the Jewis State.

197

September 17, 1982,

Despite American pressure for Israeli withdrawal from Lebanon, the Israelis felt that they had done a favor for the United States and were not being treated fairly in return.

In a move which
shocked many, Pope
John Paul II welcomed
Arafat to the Vatican,
heedless of the blood of
thousands of Christians
slaughtered in Lebanon
by the PLO.

September 24, 1982

October 1, 1982

The Arab governments
met in Fez, Morocco, to
discuss the Lebanese
debacle. They were
unable to agree among
themselves on a policy
to help defend the PLO.

199

October 8, 1982

The Begin Government's refusal to
investigate the massacre of Palestinians by
Christians in Beirut created a storm at
home and abroad.

It seemed to many that a double standard was being applied to Israel in the wake of general indifference to many a previous massacre by Arabs of their own people.

October 15, 1982

President Gamayel appeared before the U.N. Assembly and denounced Israel, whose armies had freed his country from the PLO.

October 22, 1982,

201

'BROTHERLY' ACT

Arafat and Hussein met to decide on a common policy towards Israel and the American peace proposals.

November 12, 1982

THE SCALE OF DEMOCRACY

COMMISSION OF INQUIRY

Pressure from within Israel finally led to the creation of a commission headed by leading Israeli justices.

December 3, 1982

November 19, 1982

The Western leaders continued to plead
with a battered Arafat to utter the magic
word "Israel," so they could recognize him.

The Israeli economy, badly weakened by the Lebanon war, became more and more dependent upon American assistance, leaving Jerusalem open to pressure from Washington.

December 10, 1982

Gradually it became evident that many of the thousands of terrorists who had been evacuated from Beirut were finding their way back to the PLO camps in northern Lebanon.

December 17, 1982

King Hussein's visit to
Washington was a part
of the Reagan Plan to
bring Jordan directly to
the peace process.

December 24, 1982

As a result of pressure
from Syria and Saudi
Arabia, Lebanon resisted
Israel's demand for
signing of a peace treaty.

December 31, 1982

Biased reporting led to an avalanche of hateful statements toward the Jewish State.

January 1, 1983

In view of the stretched out negotiations with Lebanon, the American Government attempted to set terms against Israel's interests.

January 7, 1983

January 14, 1983

As the year came to a close it was more
and more obvious that a Mid East peace
depended upon King Hussein's willingness
to enter the talks.